A Day in the Life: Rain Forest Animals

Macaw

Anita Ganeri

Heinemann Library
Chicago, IL

www.heinemannraintree.com
Visit our website to find out more information about Heinemann-Raintree books.

To order:
☎ Phone 888-454-2279
🖥 Visit www.heinemannraintree.com to browse our catalog and order online.

Edited by Nancy Dickmann, Rebecca Rissman, and Catherine Veitch
Designed by Steve Mead
Picture research by Mica Brancic
Originated by Capstone Global Library
Printed and bound in China by South China Printing Company Ltd

14 13 12 11 10
10 9 8 7 6 5 4 3 2 1

Library of Congress Cataloging-in-Publication Data
Ganeri, Anita, 1961-
  Macaw / Anita Ganeri.
    p. cm.—(A day in the life: rain forest animals)
  Includes bibliographical references and index.
  ISBN 978-1-4329-4105-5 (hc)—ISBN 978-1-4329-4116-1 (pb) 1. Macaws—Juvenile literature. I. Title.
  QL696.P7G36 2011
  598.7'1—dc22   2010000960

Acknowledgements
We would like to thank the following for permission to reproduce photographs: Alamy pp. 14, 23 flock (© Wildlife GmbH); Ardea p. 11 (Andrea Florence); Corbis pp. 5 (© Ted Horowitz), 9 (Science Faction/© Stuart Westmorland), 18, 19, 20, 21, 23 roost (© Frans Lanting); FLPA pp. 7 (Minden Pictures/Tim Fitzharris), 12 (Minden Pictures/Pete Oxford), 13, 23 rubbery (© Frans Lanting); Photolibrary pp. 4 (Picture Press/Juergen & Christine Sohns), 6 (John Warburton-Lee Photography), 10 (Superstock/Joe Vogan), 15, 23 clay (age fotostock/Morales Morales), 16 (Robin Smith), 17, 23 toucan (Oxford Scientific (OSF)/Carol Farneti Foster), 22 (imagebroker.net/jspix jspix); Shutterstock p. 23 rain forest (© Szefei).

Cover photograph of a red macaw parrot reproduced with permission of Corbis (Brand X/© Steve Allen).

Back cover photographs of (left) a macaw's wing reproduced with permission of Photolibrary (Picture Press/Juergen & Christine Sohns); and (right) a macaw's claw reproduced with permission of FLPA (Minden Pictures/Tim Fitzharris).

We would like to thank Michael Bright for his invaluable help in the preparation of this book.

Every effort has been made to contact copyright holders of material reproduced in this book. Any omissions will be rectified in subsequent printings if notice is given to the publisher.

All the Internet addresses (URLs) given in this book were valid at the time of going to press. However, due to the dynamic nature of the Internet, some addresses may have changed, or sites may have changed or ceased to exist since publication. While the author and publisher regret any inconvenience this may cause readers, no responsibility for any such changes can be accepted by either the author or the publisher.

Contents

Some words are in bold, **like this**. You can find them in the glossary on page 23.

What Is a Macaw?

beak

wing

A macaw is a kind of bird.

All birds have wings and beaks and bodies that are covered in feathers.

Macaws belong to a group of birds known as parrots.

Macaws can be many different colors.

What Do Macaws Look Like?

Macaws have brightly colored feathers.

It is not easy to see them among the leaves and fruit of the **rain forest** trees.

claw

Macaws use their strong toes and sharp claws to grip branches.

They use their large, curved beaks to eat food.

Where Do Macaws Live?

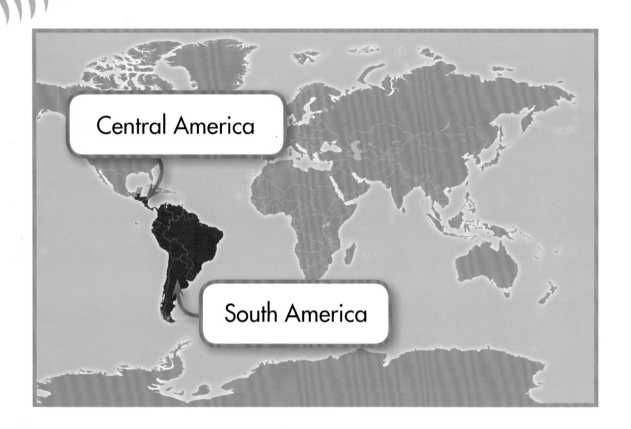

Central America

South America

Macaws live in the **rain forests** of Central America and South America.

It is warm and wet in the rain forest all year long.

In the rain forest, macaws live among the trees and along the riverbanks.

Some types of macaws live on mountains and in grasslands.

What Do Macaws Do During the Day?

Macaws usually wake up just before the sun rises.

They clean their feathers with their beaks and call to tell one another where they are.

Then the macaws fly away to find some fruit trees and start feeding.

At midday, they rest in the shade and then feed again in the afternoon.

What Do Macaws Eat?

Macaws mainly eat fruit, nuts, seeds, flowers, and leaves.

They also eat small animals, such as insects and snails.

tongue

A macaw can hold a nut in its foot and crush the shell with its strong beak.

It gets the nut out using its beak and **rubbery** tongue.

Do Macaws Live in Groups?

Macaws live in large groups called **flocks**.

During the day, the flock flies together to look for food.

clay

Sometimes, the flock may fly to a cliff by a river and eat the **clay** soil.

The clay helps a macaw's body take in the food it needs.

What Do Macaws Sound Like?

Macaws make loud screeching and squawking sounds.

The sounds help them to keep in touch with one another.

toucan

Macaws also call to warn one another of danger.

Enemies such as **toucans** like to eat the macaws' eggs and chicks.

Where Are Baby Macaws Born?

A female macaw lays her eggs in a nest inside a hollow tree.

She sits on the eggs until they hatch.

chick

When the chicks hatch, their parents take care of them and bring them food.

Later, the chicks grow flight feathers and learn to fly.

What Do Macaws Do at Night?

In the evening, macaws fly to trees to **roost**.

They squabble and squawk as they figure out where to sit.

The macaws fluff out their feathers to keep warm.

Then they sleep through the night.

Macaw Body Map

wing

feathers

eye

beak

foot

tail

Glossary

 **clay** kind of soil

 **flock** large group of birds

 **rain forest** thick forest with very tall trees and a lot of rain

 **roost** sit on a branch and go to sleep

 **rubbery** soft and bendable

 **toucan** rain forest bird with a large, colorful beak

Find Out More

Books

Catala, Ellen. *Animals in Danger*. Bloomington, MN: Yellow
   Umbrella Books, 2006.
Longenecker, Theresa. *Who Grows Up in the Rain Forest?*
   Minneapolis: Picture Window Books, 2003.

Websites

www.sandiegozoo.org/animalbytes/t-macaw.html
www.belizezoo.org/zoo/zoo/birds/mac/mac1.html
www.itsnature.org/endangered/moderately/hyacinth-macaws/

Index